I0815499

★★★★★

MLB TEAMS

San Francisco GIANTS

KENNY ABDO

Fly!
An Imprint of Abdo Zoom
abdobooks.com

abdobooks.com

Published by Abdo Zoom, a division of ABDO, P.O. Box 398166, Minneapolis, Minnesota 55439.

Printed in the United States of America, North Mankato, Minnesota.
102025
012026

Photo Credits: Alamy, Getty Images, Shutterstock
Production Contributors: Kenny Abdo, Jennie Forsberg, Grace Hansen
Design Contributors: Candice Keimig, Neil Klinepier

Library of Congress Control Number: 2025936811

Publisher's Cataloging-in-Publication Data

Names: Abdo, Kenny, author.
Title: San Francisco Giants / by Kenny Abdo
Description: Minneapolis, Minnesota : Abdo Zoom, 2026 | Series: MLB teams | Includes online resources and index.
Identifiers: ISBN 9798384940319 (lib. bdg.) | ISBN 9798384941071 (ebook) | ISBN 9798384941453 (read-to-me ebook)
Subjects: LCSH: San Francisco Giants (Baseball team)--Juvenile literature. | Baseball teams--Juvenile literature. | Professional sports--Juvenile literature. | Sports franchises--Juvenile literature. | Major League Baseball (Organization)--Juvenile literature.
Classification: DDC 796.357--dc23

Table of CONTENTS

GIANTS

A thick fog may cover San Francisco, but the Giants' history shines bright enough to light up the whole Bay!

From towering talent to World Series wins, the Giants have proven they can play the game on an **epic** scale!

Giants
2
YASTRZEMSKI
5

BATTER UP!

The Giants got their start in 1883 as the New York Gothams. They were one of the early teams in the **National League** (**NL**). As early as 1885, the team began to be known as the Giants.

The Giants won five World Series in New York before deciding to move west. The team made San Francisco their new home in 1958.

The Giants were a powerhouse in the **NL**. Willie Mays led the way for the team to reach greatness. From 1959 to 1961, he hit over 100 home runs and stole more than 50 bases, making him one of the biggest stars in baseball!

FRANCISCO

In 1962, stars such as Willie McCovey and Juan Marichal kept the team strong. McCovey hit 20 home runs and Marichal won 18 games. The hot streak led the team to the World Series! Sadly, the Giants fell to the Yankees in a close Game 7.

GRAND SLAMS

Though the Giants had many great players during the 1970s and 1980s, the team still did not win a World Series title. In 1989, the Giants finally made their return to the World Series.

The ’89 Series is known for the big earthquake that took place just before Game 3. It caused a lot of damage to San Francisco. Ten days later, Game 3 finally took place. The Oakland A’s went on to win in four games.

The Giants built up a strong roster during the 2000s. In 2001, Barry Bonds hit 73 home runs, a **record** that still stands. In 2002, the team reached the World Series but lost in seven games. Tim Lincecum joined the team in 2007, bringing fresh energy to the mound. He won the **Cy Young Award** in 2008 and 2009.

55

16
WORLD SERIES

In 2010, the Giants won their first World Series since moving to San Francisco. The team beat the Rangers in five games. Édgar Rentería hit a three-run homer and was named World Series MVP.

The Giants remained larger than life with two more World Series wins in 2012 and 2014! Pablo Sandoval hit three home runs in Game 1 of the 2012 World Series.

In 2014, Madison Bumgarner threw 21 innings, allowed only one run, and won Series MVP. It was one of the strongest runs in modern baseball.

The Giants were back in the playoffs in 2016 but lost a tough playoff **NL Division** Series to the Cubs. After four losing seasons, the team surprised everyone in 2021 with 107 wins, a team **record**.

Buster Posey also had an **All-Star** season. Posey **retired** after the team lost in the 2021 playoffs. It was time for a new generation of Bay Area stars to restore the glory.

HALL OF FAME

Willie Mays was a superstar who made everything on the field look easy. He hit 646 home runs with the Giants and won two MVP awards. He made 24 **All-Star** teams and was known for his basket catches and daring base running. Mays was named to the Baseball Hall of Fame in 1979.

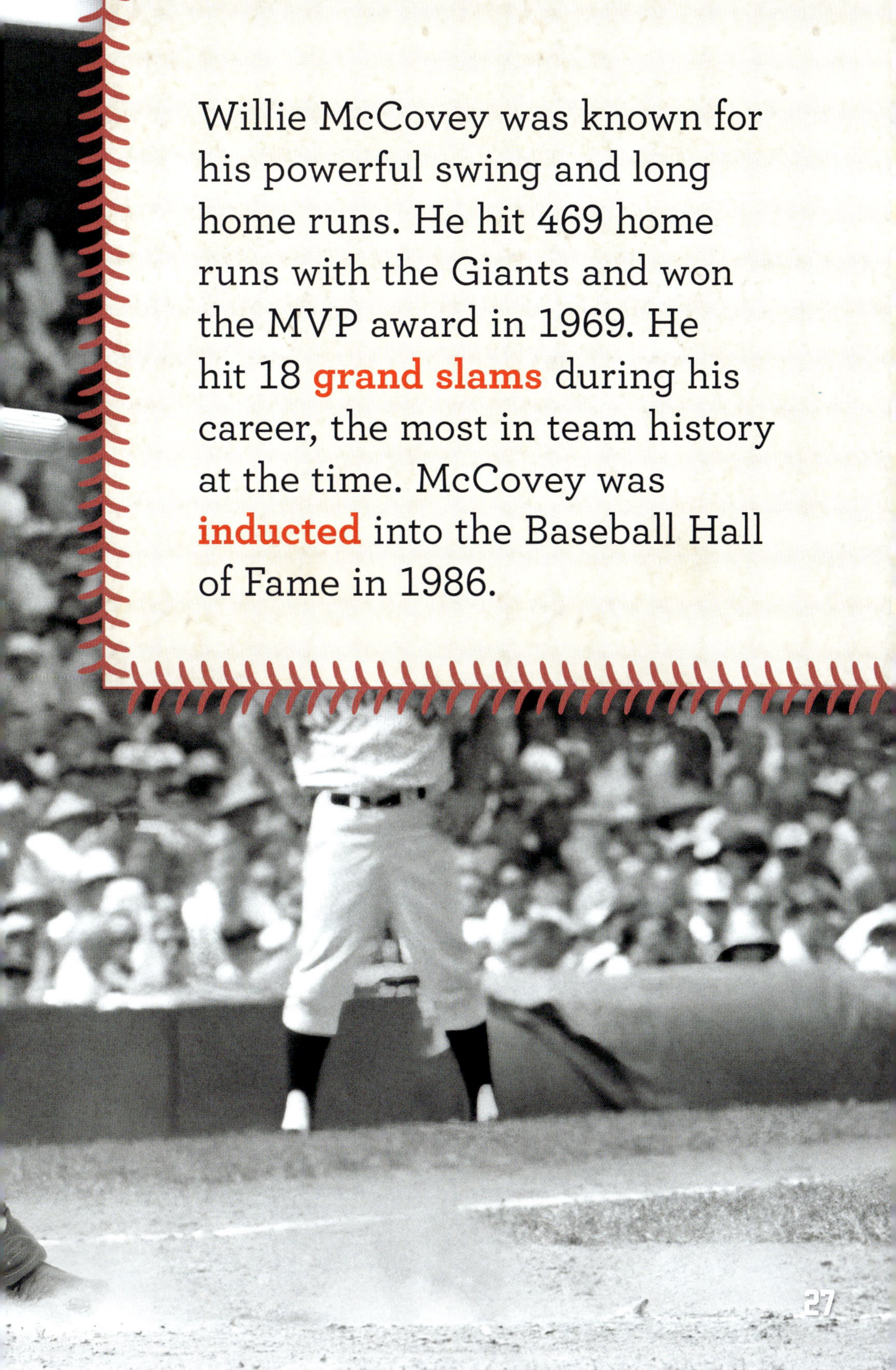

Willie McCovey was known for his powerful swing and long home runs. He hit 469 home runs with the Giants and won the MVP award in 1969. He hit 18 **grand slams** during his career, the most in team history at the time. McCovey was **inducted** into the Baseball Hall of Fame in 1986.

With seven MVP awards under his belt, Barry Bonds could crush a baseball like no one else. Bonds was a one-man show in 2001, hitting home runs at a historic pace. When Bonds left the Giants, he held many team **records**, including 586 home runs. Bonds ended his career with 762 home runs, the most in Major League Baseball history.

GLOSSARY

All-Star – a team consisting of athletes chosen as the best at their positions from all teams in a league or region.

Cy Young Award – an annual American baseball award given to the best pitcher in each of the two MLB leagues.

division – a number of teams grouped together in a sport for competitive purposes.

epic – unusually great in size.

grand slam – a home run hit when all three bases are occupied by base runners, resulting in four runs scored.

inducted – brought in as a member.

National League (NL) – one of two 15-team leagues that make up MLB.

record – the top achievement by a team or player that no one has done before.

retire – to leave one's job and stop working.

ONLINE RESOURCES

To learn more about the San Francisco Giants, please visit **abdobooklinks.com** or scan this QR code. These links are routinely monitored and updated to provide the most current information available.

INDEX